101 MONEY-MAKING IDEAS FOR "SAHM"S

by

Cynthia MacGregor

Roundtable Publishing – all rights reserved

www.roundtablepublishinginc.com

ISBN: 978-1-63039-037-2

For Laurel…of course

A Few Words to the Wise...and the Wives

Whether they're not working because they're home-schooling their kids, or they're taking a number of years off from their careers to raise their not-yet-school-age children, or for whatever other reason, there seems to be a growing number of women who describe themselves as "SAHM"s—stay-at-home moms.

But many of these women, even though they're not in urgent need of bringing in a second income, could still benefit from having some additional money.

• It might mean the difference between Hamburger Helper or steak for dinner some nights.

• It might be the means by which you can start your children's college fund.

• It might be the means of building up your "emergency fund," saving faster toward your next family vacation, or even saving for your dream house, or the new addition to your current home.

• Or the extra money you earn might be your "fun money," with which you treat yourself (or your whole family) to a few luxuries or frivolities that you wouldn't in good conscience carve out of your budget but can happily spend money on when the money is "extra" income you've earned.

Okay, we've established that, whether or not you *need* extra income, it's certainly good to have it. And when we get to the heart of this book—the hundred and one ways to earn extra income that the book's title promised you—we'll talk about the actual ideas. But first things first. (How many times have you said *that* to your kids?!)

The first thing, in this case, is to decide that you really are serious about earning some extra money in your (laughably little) free time. The next thing is to decide just how much time you actually have to spare for a money-making venture, and *when*. That is, is your availability:

• From 9 to 3 while the kids are in school?

• From 1 to 2 when the baby naps?

• For an hour or two every day while your home-schooled kids study independently?

• On a catch-as-catch-can basis when your kids are playing quietly?

• On Monday, Wednesday, and Friday mornings, while your three-year-old is at the play gym, or five afternoons a week while he's in pre-school?

• Whenever the teenager next door is free to supervise your toddler so you can work?

• After 5:30, when your husband is home and can take over?

• Evenings, when the kids are in bed?

It helps, in planning a money-making enterprise, to know how much time you can realistically devote to it, what time of day that is, and whether you can plan on a regular schedule of availability or not.

The next question you need to ask yourself is how much money you have available to put into your venture, if any. Depending on what you choose to do, you may need to buy materials, or pay for advertising, or incur some other nominal business expense.

The last question you need to ask yourself for now is what your talents and abilities are. I'll bet that when you go through the list of money-making ideas, you'll find some that apply to you and appeal to you but that you hadn't thought of on your own. Still, it helps if you start with an idea or two of where your strengths lie. Are you an excellent baker? Do you speak fluent French? Are you a talented painter or sketch artist, knitter or quilter? Are you highly organized? Are you very persuasive? One of those abilities or skills or strengths of yours may be the key to your earning extra income—perhaps even in a way that isn't one of the hundred and one this book offers.

At the end of the hundred and one ideas, there's a little more information for you on setting up your business, finding extra time, being businesslike, and a few similar matters. But for now, let's look at those hundred and one ideas I've promised you. Some are for more formal albeit very part-time businesses. Some are for simply earning a little extra money now and then. Some are so much fun they'll hardly feel like you're working. Some are for services for which you'll only occasionally get a call and will bring in only a little money from time to time, while others have the potential to grow into full-time businesses once the kids have grown old enough for you to work full time, if you care to.

Which one (or ones) will appeal most to *you*?

101 Money-Making Ideas

1 – Run a shopping service for shut-ins (or anyone short of time).

Your prime candidates for this service are the older or incapacitated residents of your community, people who no longer drive, who don't get around easily or at all, anyone whose health situation is such that they would have trouble getting to the supermarket or drugstore. (This would also include people with emotional health issues, or such phobias as agoraphobia.) But you might find that overworked people of both sexes, newly divorced or widowed men, and others would appreciate a weekly food service.

You can charge a lower fee for regularly weekly trips, ganging up all your customers' orders at one time, and a higher fee for special trips, making runs to the supermarket or drugstore on demand.

2 – Sell advertising by phone for your local newspaper.

If they're not willing to pay you by the hour, will they pay you on a commission basis to make phone calls soliciting advertising space sales in their pages? Contact them! If there's a local weekly or something else other than your big daily, they're even more likely to need your services.

3 - Scavenge for perfectly good or almost-perfectly good items that have been put out at curbside for pick-up, and resell them.

It's amazing the number of items put out at curbside for garbage collection that are in very usable shape. Whoever first said we live in a disposable economy certainly hit the nail on the head. But one family's loss can be another family's gain. So if you see (as I did recently) a child's toy horse on springs that's in perfectly fine condition, a bookshelf, an end table, or any other item that you could "rescue," perhaps store in your garage temporarily, and possibly touch up with paint or effect any other small needed repair, bring it home, and resell it—either "as is" or slightly refurbished.

Where to resell it? At a local consignment shop that handles household goods, at a yard sale, or through a "miscellaneous household goods" ad in a Pennysaver or other publication that's inexpensive to place an ad in.

4 – Organize and "de-clutter" people's closets, kitchens, or offices.

I once met a woman who made a full-time living doing exactly this in people's homes. And I once was hired for several days' work in organizing an office's filing system. There are lots of disorganized people out there, and plenty of them will pay someone to come in.

If you're the kind of person who can look at a plastic tackle box and see it as a super container for earrings, who can think of a much better means of arranging an herb-and-spice rack than alphabetically, who sees tackling a cluttered closet and organizing it as a joyous challenge, this is the venture for you.

5 – Turn your knitting, crocheting, quilting, or needlepoint into a money-making venture.

Do you like to "make things"? Are you forever knitting sweaters and crocheting Afghans? Are you running out of friends and relatives to gift with your creations?

Sell them! You can knit or crochet to order, or you can craft things in advance and then sell them afterward, or both. (Obviously it's easier to sell a pre-made afghan, where only the color is an issue, not size, than it is to sell a pre-made sweater. But knit caps or crocheted ponchos don't require such accurate sizing as do sweaters.)

6 – Organize scrapbooks for people whose mementoes are stuffed in a shoebox.

Scrapbooking has become quite an art of its own, and you can carry this particular enterprise far beyond simply preserving paper mementoes in scrapbooks with magnetic pages. Of course, some people will want you to do just that and nothing more. But others will appreciate all the decorative touches you can add…and the more you add, the more you can charge.

7 – Prepare weekly deliveries of a week's worth of meals for people who are either time-challenged, physically challenged, or simply culinary challenged.

Your customers can include overworked people with no time to cook, the elderly or physically disabled, or people who simply don't know how to cook or don't like to. To cut down your work, you'll deliver a week's worth of foods every week, all frozen, which they can defrost and nuke one of nightly. You may choose to deliver a complete dinner or simply a main course, leaving it to your customers to supply the side dishes. You can do all your cooking in one long day, or a little every day.

You may need to buy a second freezer for this particular venture. Buying used is more economical.

You should charge extra if someone has a particular dietary need (e.g. low-salt, Kosher, fat-free, gluten-free, dairy-free).

8 – Be a photographer.

Nowadays almost everyone has a camera, whether digital or old-fashioned. But simply having the equipment does not insure you're getting good pictures. There's more to photography than pointing and shooting. It's a matter of composition, of getting your subject to pose nicely or catching your subject unposed at just the right moment, and of course such questions as lighting.

If you're truly good with a camera, you can take pictures of babies, family functions (don't think just of wedding photography—what about Sweet Sixteens, Quinceañeros, and large reunions?), and organizations (Scout Troops, Little Leagues, church youth groups, etc.).

In the case of organizations, you will want to offer a percentage of the revenue from every sold picture to the organization.

You can also take pictures at business functions (retirement parties, corporate anniversaries, ribbon-cutting ceremonies).

9 – Babysit other people's kids.

Whether you run an in-home daycare center or playgroup and have the same five kids over every morning or every day, or whether you simply make yourself available on an as-needed basis, you can pick up extra money by watching other people's kids while you're home taking care of your own.

10 – Teach evening classes for adults.

In my area, the public schools offer evening classes for adults, which are taught by knowledgeable members of the community, who need not be certified teachers. As well, two of the local towns have recreation departments under whose auspice's classes are offered. People teaching in the schools at night are paid by the hour; people teaching through the recreation departments are paid by the student. Either way, the point is that they are paid.

But of course, whether or not you have such an opportunity in your community, you can still give classes. If the classes are small, and you are not uncomfortable having strangers in your home, you can do that. Otherwise, you may be able to rent a meeting room from a local organization at a nominal fee.

11 – Relieve the agony of "de feet."

Even people who wouldn't ever pay for a full pedicure may be happy for someone who'll just clip their toenails. If a person is older, heavy, arthritic, visually challenged, or otherwise has difficulty clipping his or her own toenails, and especially if that person doesn't live with someone who can do the task, she may be more than happy to pay for the service. And you'll charge less than a podiatrist, even less than a salon would charge. I've known several people who, unable to clip their own nails, have gone to either a podiatrist or beauty salon for that service. Wouldn't you like to earn that money yourself?

Of course, for an additional fee you can pumice calluses and/or paint toenails for your clients too.

12 – Create artificial flower arrangements.

You can sell these to individuals or to businesses. Whether you artfully fill a basket, decoratively grace a vase, or do something more clever and unique, you can create artificial flower arrangements and sell them for well more than the cost of the basic "ingredients."

You can also stock an inventory of artificial flower arrangements, if you have room, and rent them out to people who are having banquets, large birthday, anniversary, or retirement parties, weddings, and other catered functions for table decorations that will cost far less than the cost of fresh flowers for every table.

13 – You've been framed! No, it's the picture that's been framed.

And you're the one who's done it. For the average photo of the family, or that great shot you got at the ocean with your camera, a drugstore picture frame will generally do. But what of the painting bought without a frame? What of the heirloom portrait of Great-Great-Grandma, the frame of which has cracked? What of that really spectacular sunset photo that ought to be displayed in a quality frame that will set it off? These call for professional framing.

If you know how (or can learn), you can become a professional picture framer at home.

14 – Offer lessons by Email.

Whatever your forté is, if it's something you can teach at a distance, offer lessons by Email. Correspondence courses are hardly new—this is just taking it into the cyber age.

15 - If your sewing isn't "sew-sew," sew!

Whether you do alterations or make clothes from scratch, if you're handy with a needle (and a sewing machine), you can turn your talent into cash. Seamstresses can do such simple work as hemming, more complicated work such as letting out or taking in seams, or create clothes from jump.

If you don't just do alterations but actually create clothes, you have two choices: You can either choose your own patterns and fabric, select a popular size, and then sell the finished creations, or let your clients choose their own fabric and patterns, then turn these over to you to craft the finished products.

16 – Be a clown!

As the song says, "All the world loves a clown." And everyone wants to be loved, so…be a clown! Clowns work at children's birthday parties, of course, but clowns also can work at adult parties, fund-raisers, shopping center openings, day care center openings, nursery school parties, and other such opportunities.

You'll need a costume, makeup, and a routine. If you've never clowned before, get in some practice before you hire yourself out. Study other clowns and see what they do and how they do it. Then offer your services free to the local hospital's children's floor or a local children's charity to get in some practice.

Then—ta-dah!—you're ready for "the big time": a paying gig!

17 – Help people organize and write their memoirs.

Plenty of people have interesting stories to tell but no gift for writing. Still others have less fascinating stories to tell, but still their stories will interest their children, grandchildren, and beyond. Some of these people will want to try to sell their stories to publishers; others only want to preserve their stories for posterity within their families.

Some of your clients will need help only in organizing their material or in being prompted as to what to tell. Most will need you to ghostwrite the book from go to whoa. If you're an organized person with a flair for writing, and you have a computer, you have everything you need to help people preserve their life stories.

18 – Pat-a-cake, pat-a-cake, baker's man, bake me a cake as fast as you can.

Well, not as *fast* as you can but as *well* as you can. If you've got a flair for baking—and particularly if each of your cakes or pies or other delectable treats is a thing of beauty to look at as well as a joy to eat, you can sell your wares, whether they're pies, cakes, cookies, tarts, or other yummy sweets.

If you get really good at it, you can even branch out into wedding cakes—very complicated but *very* remunerative.

Start slow, though, with that devil's food, angel food, strawberry shortcake, or apple pie that's been delighting the family for years. The rewards you'll reap will be very sweet indeed.

19 – Edit for credit.

Financial credit, that is. There's plenty of opportunity in many a community for editing book manuscripts for would-be writers…or other editing assignments as well. (If you happen to live near a college, solicit work from the teachers and professors there, who may want to get a book published to increase their prestige but may not be as good at writing about their subject as they are at teaching it.)

20 – Be a menu planner.

"Now, what should I cook for dinner tonight?" That's the plaint of more people than you would believe. They don't want the same-old-same-old, they don't have great imaginations or a huge store of recipes…and they're in a quandary about what to serve for dinner. Enter…you. With recipes in hand. Plan a balanced meal for each of the seven nights of a week, provide recipes and a grocery list to cover the entire menu plan, and do it every week. And collect on your own ingenuity.

21 – Plan kids' birthday parties.

You're already an expert! You've planned your own child's parties, whether they were simple home affairs with pin-the-tail and other games, or bowling parties, or something more elaborate. Now you can take over for other moms, apply your own expertise plus a dash of ingenuity, and take the major part of the hassle out of birthday parties for the birthday child's mom by planning the party, sending out the invites, filling the goodie bags, buying the food, hiring any entertainment, organizing the games, supervising the whole thing…and hear the figurative cash register go *ka-ching* at the end of the day.

22 – Be a personal trainer.

Are you fit? Reasonably knowledgeable about exercise and eating? A good leader? You can be a top sergeant…er, uh…a personal trainer. (Is there really much difference?) "Drop and give me fifty!" Oh…mmm…you don't want to be *quite* that strong…but if you can direct a fellow human who's got a bit too much in the girth department, you can weigh in, in your pocketbook, while she weighs *out* on the scales.

23 – What branches grow on your family tree?

If you've researched your own genealogy, and you had to do a bit of digging, you may know enough about genealogy research to explore the branches of other people's family trees. You can charge more if the research is extensive, and if you're a clever genealogist who knows how to find those hidden roots and branches, people will be willing to pay for the results.

24 – Be a portrait artist.

If you have a good artistic talent, put it to good use in portraiture. Many portrait artists work from photographs, and if that's you, you'll need a good camera. This is particularly useful if you're commissioned to paint a picture of someone's prized dog or cat or horse, since it's hard to get an animal to stay still for long when you want it to…and you certainly can't bring a horse into your studio!

Of course most of your portrait subjects will be people, but don't be surprised if you're asked to paint a poodle, a terrier, a Siamese cat, or a thoroughbred mare.

25 – Don't be mad over Mad Ave…just write!

Madison Avenue was long the fabled home of Manhattan advertising agencies. (Today they're located all over the island…and in nearby areas as well.) But what does a local business owner do who can't afford Mad Ave prices? He or she turns to you!

For a modest fee…but one that will still enrich your checking account…you can write an ad (print or broadcast) for a local business that can't afford big agency prices—New York or local—but can afford to pay you a modest fee for writing an ad for their enterprise.

Got a way with words? Weigh in. Way to go!

26 – Hunt 'n' peck is a peck of trouble…so type.

Who needs typing services? Plenty of people! Believe it or not, in this computer age there are still lots of people who are sans PC or Mac, who would appreciate your typing a document for them. Then there are those who have a computer but not the typing skills and don't want to "translate" a longhand document into keyboard.

You to the rescue!

Offer to type any document, from one page to a whole book.

And charge for it!

27 - Eat at Joe's. And feed your car at Mike's. Sell ads on menus.

I had a friend who earned a living for quite a few years by selling ads on restaurant placemats. The advertisers each buy a square around the border of the placemat. Enough advertisers fill a placemat. The restaurant agrees to it in advance. The businesses buy ads. The salesman (that's you!) keeps the ad revenue, pays the printer to print the placemats, delivers them to the restaurant, delivers one copy to each advertiser...and pockets the profits.

You can do something similar with menus, as well.

Obviously, you're not going after elegant restaurants with this business. Your target customers are coffee shops, diners, "family" restaurants, and similar casual establishments.

28 – Be a life coach.

Some people need coaching in their athletics, their studies, their fitness, or other areas of their life. And some people need coaching regarding all of their life. Their life paths. Their careers. Even how to handle their relationships, not only romantic but friendly and familial. Are you a positive person who speaks with conviction, gives good advice, can give a pep talk that inspires, who knows how to motivate people and to guide them? Then you may have the potential to be a life coach, a career you can work at very part-time now and possibly even expand into full-time at a later date when your kids are older.

29 – Presto! It's magic!

We already talked about hiring out as a clown at parties, but maybe you haven't the aptitude for clowning. That doesn't mean you can't be a party entertainer, though. Have you any experience performing magic tricks?

For some reason, the overwhelming majority of magicians through the years have been male, but there's nothing about prestidigitation that favors males over females, and if you have an aptitude for performing sleight-of-hand, you can turn your talent into money...presto!

If your repertoire consists of simple, basic tricks, that's still good enough to hold an audience of four-year-olds or eight-year-olds in wide-eyed wonder. To enrapture a group of grown-ups you'll need more sophisticated tricks (and probably a more glamorous costume as well), but magic isn't solely the provenance of children's parties, and if you're good enough to entertain adults you can hire out not only to kids' birthday parties but to lodge meetings and other organizational meetings, adult parties (birthday, anniversary, retirement, farewell, bon voyage, occasion-less cocktail parties or dinner parties), and corporate functions as well.

30 – Be a party planner.

We already talked about planning and running kids' birthday parties, but there's a world of party planning on beyond the pin-the-tail or Chuck E. Cheese set. Whether it's an office party, a bar mitzvah, a lavish catered affair for no special occasion, a holiday party, a "milestone" birthday, or some other type of celebration, if you've the right skills and know-how, you can save the host or hostess the headache of supervising the details and— for a nice chunk of change—take over the hassle of making sure the party comes off perfect.

You'll need to arrange for a venue if the party's to be held somewhere other than the host's home, arrange for rental tables, chairs, utensils, and china if needed, plan decorations, send out invitations, plan a menu and either engage the services of a caterer, or hire additional temporary household help if the host plans to have his own household staff do the cooking and serving with added personnel to assist. Then there's the matter of liquor (and mixers, and perhaps rented barware, and probably a hired bartender), possibly entertainment, and other little details, such as perhaps arranging for a "gift table" on which guests can deposit gifts they are bringing for their host.

Whew! What a lot of planning! No wonder some hosts and hostesses are willing to pay a party planner to take all the hassle off their hands. Giving a large party is *work!* So let it be *your* work!

31 – Fanfare for the fare du jour—straight from your computer.

Some restaurants offer a different menu every night. Many others offer a standard menu day after day but offer daily specials, which are printed out and attach to or inserted into the regular menu. *Someone's* got to type up and print out those daily menus or daily specials…and the more attractively presented they are, the better impression the restaurant makes.

Are you competent to do simple graphics on your computer? Make up several samples of attractive-looking full menus and "specials" menus, then show these around to local restaurant managers. (Hint: Don't run more than one sample out on plain white paper. Use mock parchment or other attractive papers for the remaining samples.) You can approach everything from haute cuisine palaces to diners. Offer to deliver daily, in whatever quantity they specify. All they need to supply you with is the copy (words) to go on the menus. You'll take care of the rest, keying in the words, choosing an attractive yet easily readable font, decorating the page just a bit if the management wants it, running out as many copies as management desires, and delivering the new menus daily.

32 – Nail down some income…by doing nails.

Are you a manicurist…or could you do simple polishing, shaping, and cuticle work, even if you can't do acrylics? You can set up a small corner of the family room as a nail salon and service a select number of customers at mutually convenient times.

33 – Be a grief counsellor.

Again, as I said in the item above, if a person seems suicidal or otherwise seriously emotionally troubled, it's time for a mental health professional. But the average person who's grieving over a recently deceased friend or relative may need a little more help than his or her friends can give yet isn't in a mental crisis. You can let him know it's all right to cry. You can help him work through his grief. And you can help him find ways to make himself feel better. Will it help him to write a letter to the person who died, saying all the things he never said while he had the chance? Will it help him to revisit places he went to with that person? Will it help him just to talk about the person? Does he need to watch a good three-hankie movie to release the tears? Will a dinner of comfort foods soothe his soul? Sometimes a dinner of mashed potatoes and meatloaf is a "recipe" for healing a hurt.

If you're an empathetic person who likes to help and who knows the ways to deal with grief, this may be an opportunity for you.

34 – Teach practical self-defense classes to women and/or to kids.

Though you may want to throw in a few good martial arts moves, the bulk of your lessons will focus on other maneuvers…including common-sense defensive actions to keep people from getting attacked in the first place. (Stress that if your students avoid doing the things that can lead them to become victims, they may not need to know how to deliver a karate chop.) I am speaking of such self-defensive actions as checking the back seat and floor of your car before you get into it, having a co-worker or security guard escort you to your car if you're parked in an office building's garage and have worked late, and not pulling over to the side of the road if bumped from behind in a deserted spot, or at very least not getting out of your car. (Preferably drive to an area where there are plenty of people, or at very least summon help from the police using your cellphone.)

Other than martial arts moves, there are three maneuvers that can temporarily incapacitate most attackers. I think most women know that kneeing an attacking male in the crotch will temporarily put him out of action. Unfortunately, most attacking males also know that women have been taught this for many generations, so they're prepared to defend themselves there. Too, some women are squeamish about kneeing a man there. Another very useful counter-attack maneuver is to form a V with the index and middle fingers and jab at the attacker's eyes. Even if you connect with only one of them, he'll be out of action for a bit. The third maneuver is to take the heel of your palm and aim for the attacker's nostrils, pushing swiftly upward as if to push his nose into his forehead.

35 – Craft earrings…and sell them.

If you have an artistic or crafty flair, why not fashion unusual, distinctive earrings? You can sell to friends (and friends of friends of friends), or through local stores such as hair salons or clothing stores, or at earring parties (think Tupperware parties…but sell earrings instead, gifting each party hostess with a couple of pairs of earrings for having you over to talk to her friends). You can even put classified ads in the paper advertising your wares and promoting one-of-a-kind earrings or earrings made to order.

36 – With a clip, clip, here, and a clip, clip there...be a dog groomer (or washer).

If you're used to giving your own dog his "haircuts" or have ever had dog grooming experience, you can also groom dogs for other people. Or simply be a dog-washer and take over a chore that many people hate.

37 – Mistress Mary, quite contrary, how does your herb garden grow?

This spring, instead of putting in zucchini and wondering whom to give it all away to, plant herbs...and decide whom to sell them to! (You may even be able to sell them all to a small local market.) Over the winter, you can grow a modest number of herbs in indoor pots, as well. Fresh herbs confer a marvelous flavor to foods, but not every cook has a green thumb...or the space to grow herbs in. That's where you come in...and where the profits come in.

38 – Handpaint distinctive vases.

Buy inexpensive plain but not cheap-looking vases and decorate them with paint. Then resell them at a considerable markup. (Don't overlook the possibility of selling some to your local florists and gift shops as well as to individuals.)

39 – "Wrap-sody" in blue...be a gift wrapper.

Though the holiday season will doubtless be your busiest time, people all year round give gifts for birthdays, weddings, and other occasions. They like the gifts to make a good appearance when first presented, yet not everyone is handy with gift-wrapping. If the present was purchased at a store that offers free gift-wrapping, all well and good for the buyer/giver. But many stores don't offer that service; many others do a minimal job of it; and then there are gifts that didn't come from a store. They were either homemade gifts or "back of the closet" (i.e. "recycled") gifts. Too, some gifts are harder to wrap than others. A book? Easy. An umbrella? Not so easy!

With a good assortment of wrapping papers, ribbons, and bows, including wrapping papers suitable for kids and masculine-looking papers, as well as papers themed to special occasions (e.g.

birthdays, Christmas, Chanukah), you're set to earn money as a "wrap artist"!

For an additional fee, if you want, you can then wrap the present in an over-layer of brown mailing wrap, label it, and take it to the Post Office or UPS station, saving your client from standing in line.

40 – "Tell me a *personalized* story"

Write a number of original children's stories, and/or poems, and/or songs. Offer for sale a personalized cassette with a story on each side, or several poems, or several songs, each one mentioning the child by name as the hero/heroine of the story. You will have to record each cassette individually, since each one will have a different name for the child who's the hero or heroine. (And some will say "he" while some will say "she.") But you have to write each story or song or poem only once.

When selling each cassette, make sure to mention that you have other stories available in the series, so if Michael or Andrea is thrilled to be the star of a story all about him or her, you can sell his or her mom another cassette with different stories (or poems or songs, or a mixture of all of these) in which Andrea or Michael is once again the star.

41 – Write parodies to order.

Though they're not technically parodies, that's what they're often called. I'm referring to lyrics set to other people's music, which are often used at "roasts" and at banquets honoring people, as well as at other parties and occasions. Whether someone is retiring, moving away, having a milestone birthday, being installed as lodge president, or being feted for some other reason, a part of the festivities may well include a song being sung to and about the guest of honor.

And someone has to write the song. For the right fee, that someone could be you.

42 – "Matchmaker, matchmaker, make me a match."

So sang Tevye's daughter in *Fiddler on the Roof*. And matchmakers aren't a bygone service. Modern-day men and women use dating services, both local and Internet. Matchmaking is simply a more personalized form of dating service. Instead of having your clients fill out forms, you interview them in person and get a feel for what kind of people they are and what kind of people they'd pair well with.

Of course, if you're nervous about having strangers come to your house, you could still do your interview by questionnaire and by phone.

43 – Logo design.

If you've got a flair for artistic design, you can design logos for companies either locally or even globally. Since reaching companies out of area requires either a great deal of postage or else resorting to Email spamming, you're best off starting with local firms. A strong, unique logo that catches the eye and lodges in the memory is very helpful to any business (including yours! Show off your ability by designed the best darned logo you can for yourself!).

44 – Be a research assistant.

Who needs a research assistant? Authors, professors, and businesspeople, for starters. Now you know whom to aim your advertising at. Your clients needn't be local; you can easily transmit your research results to someone out of area via Email or "snail-mail." If you're good at looking up information, sell that talent to people who are less good at ferreting out the info they need (or simply haven't got the time to do it).

As a bonus, you'll learn lots of new information in the course of your digging.

45 – Be a "reminder service."

Whether he uses an old-fashioned calendar or datebook or the newest modern electronic device, it won't do your prospective client any good if he doesn't remember to look at it. And believe it or not, there are still plenty of people out there who forget upcoming significant dates till it's too late. Then it's, "Oops! Rats! Forgot Mom's birthday again!"

For a small fee, you can make a phone call or send an Email reminding your clients of each significant date—either a week in advance, so they can send a card or gift to arrive in time, or on the actual date in question, if all that's needed to acknowledge the occasion is a phone call on the date of the birthday or other special occasion.

Of course, besides birthdays, anniversaries, and other such occasions, you can offer to remind your clients of any other dates they need to be kept from forgetting as well. They may want to be reminded when it's time to reset their clocks for Daylight Savings Time and Standard Time, to be reminded a week in advance of April 15 Income Tax Deadline, or at any other times of their choosing.

46 – A soft or cheery voice is a much better rooster than a radio.

Though nobody likes being wakened from a sound sleep (or a pleasant dream) by a ringing phone, an alarm clock or clock radio is often a far worse alternative. Set the clock radio to a classical station at a soft volume, and you run the risk of not hearing it at all. Set it to a rock station at full blast, and you'll wake up for sure, but you'll start the day on edge.

So how about waking up to a soft or cheery voice…yours? For a fee, you can play alarm clock to your clients, waking each one up at the designated time, staying on the line for a sentence or two to be sure your client is upright and won't go back to sleep, wishing him or her a good morning, and starting the morning off for your client much better and much more kindly than any clock radio or ringing or buzzing alarm can.

47 – Be a slogan writer.

A catchy slogan is a useful thing for most any business to have. It helps potential customers remember the name of the company, or remember what their chief product or service is. But the fellow or gal who's so excellent at repairing cars, baking cakes, filling out tax forms, or selling clothes for your child may not have the needed creativity to dream up a clever, catchy slogan.

Do you?

If you do, you can sell your services as a slogan-writer. Start with local businesses, of course. You can always try to expand beyond your own area once you've exhausted the possibilities there.

48 – A tutor isn't someone who blows a horn.

But you can "toot your own horn" about how knowledgeable you are at French, calculus, geography, or reading, and it just might get you some clients who need extra study help.

The old expression is, "Those who can, do. Those who can't, teach." But we all know that many teachers can do well the things they teach.

Your clients may be kids or adults. Many parents are only too happy to pay someone who can help young Pat to master the intricacies of a tough class, whether it's French, geometry, or geography. Though if your forté is a foreign language, you might find yourself teaching adults. People who are about to go overseas on business or pleasure often want to immerse themselves in French, Spanish, Greek, Italian, or Russian, as the case may be. Or you may find yourself helping semi-literate adults to read, or teaching art to aspiring artists.

Whatever your personal knowledge, share it one-on-one with students who need tutoring. People seeking private lessons are generally willing to pay more for individual instruction than people taking group lessons. Go for it!

49 – Be a gift shopper.

You may love shopping, but trust me, there are plenty of people who hate it. (I'm one of those.) And then there are those folks who don't actually hate shopping; they're just flummoxed at the prospect of picking out a gift for Aunt Agatha, or for that friend who has everything or who is so hard to please. If the budget permits, they'd be only too glad to pay someone to do their shopping for them.

That's your cue to enter stage left, offer your services, and proceed immediately to the local mall…or to a little store you know of that sells wonderful, innovative gifts…or to dredge out your stock of offbeat catalogues, if there's time enough to mail-order a gift before the occasion rolls around.

Your client gets the credit for picking out such a divine, perfect gift. But that's all right. He or she gets the credit, but you get the cash!

50 – Where's the party…platter?

Many a caterer has gotten his or her start working from a home kitchen. But if your present kitchen, or your present family circumstances, preclude your offering all-out catering services, you can still offer party platters. These are suitable for cocktail parties, casual parties, office "do"s, and other festivities for which all that's needed is finger sandwiches, or dips, or hors d'oeuvres.

From parmesan-spinach dip to turkey and pesto on rye to chicken wings to mini meatballs to…well, *you* dream up the menu. And then drum up the customers. If they want something more than just onion dip (yawnnnn), or they're looking for something more creative (or less expensive) than the local caterers offer, you can step in and fill the bill…and your bank account.

51 – Friend-match.

A friend-match puts potential friends together the way a dating service puts potential couples together. People who are new in town, who don't open up to strangers easily, whose jobs don't give them the opportunity to meet other people, or who are "socially challenged" are all your potential customers.

You can match up friends on the basis of shared interests, compatible intellect, complementary personalities, or simple intuitiveness on your part.

Sometimes having a good friend is even more important than having a marvelous Significant Other.

52 – Finishing touches—seasonal decorations for homes and offices.

I have a friend whose house is always decorated for the season. Whether it's fresh flowers or pine cones, turkeys or Santas, vases full of autumn leaves or paper snowflakes, she has something appropriate to the season displayed at all times…and she never leaves a display out for more than a month or two. And since her business is located in her home, her clients get to see the display as well as her friends. (Though she had such displays even when she didn't have an in-home office.)

Many offices put up seasonal decorations for Thanksgiving and the winter holidays, but most don't take the trouble to carry it through all year. But some do…and others would if given the opportunity to do so for an affordable fee without having to put thought and effort into it themselves.

Plenty of individuals too would decorate their home thematically for the seasons if they didn't have to put time and thought and effort into it.

That's where you come into the picture. Offer your "seasonal decorating services" to both businesses and individuals, for whom you'll provide anything from fresh flowers to autumn leaves to decorative Santas to colorful ears of Indian corn to artificial flower arrangements (yeh, they're fake, but they'll last longer than a week), to...well, what can *you* find in your area (or by mail order) that will grace your clients' homes or offices? Cattails? Artificial snow? Pussywillow? Christmas balls?

It's the finishing touch to your clients' office reception area, home entry hall or living room, or...?

53 – Babysitter registry.

When's the last time *you* tried to find a sitter on a Saturday night? You'll have the edge if the sitters in the area all register with you...and you'll make a profit too. Desperate parents will absolutely love you...and you'll absolutely love the profits.

54 – Offer "crafts hours" or "messy hours" for kids.

You already keep your own kids busy with clay or fingerpaints or construction paper or whatever kind of projects you involve them in. Why not involve other kids as well...and make a profit from their busy fingers?

Think up some projects on beyond what the average mom would have available for her kids. Then offer these projects to other kids for an hour at a time...and charge the moms for "crafts class" or "projects group" or "messy hour" or whatever you want to call your enterprise.

You'll need a family room, basement, or other large area where you can seat five to ten kids besides yours, as well as one parent for each, and where it won't matter if things get a wee bit messy...or more than just a wee bit.

You can offer this every Saturday afternoon, once a month, every day after school, or every day during the day for the pre-school set, or on any other schedule that suits you.

This is not a babysitting service. The moms will stay and chat with each other during the hour their kids are involved in their projects. It's the moms' responsibility to keep the kids in line, if anyone gets out of hand. Your responsibility is to provide the needed materials, explain today's project, and give help to anyone who needs it.

55 – Make sales calls for a local business.

If you're willing to work for straight commission, it will be easier to persuade a local enterprise (perhaps a photo studio or cleaning service or house painter) to give you a chance. If you're holding out for a guaranteed salary or draw, you'll need to be more persuasive—and very businesslike—to convince your new employer to hire you to work at home and get paid for your time. But if you're very persuasive when you talk to your potential employer, he or she may see that you'd be good at what you propose to do. If you can "sell" him or her, you can sell future clients too!

Plenty of companies and individuals, from baby photographers to car dealerships, need phone callers to try to make sales…or simply to make the initial contact. Call local businesses that are likely to need callers and offer to be their initial caller or their total salesman, turning over qualified leads to their sales team or making the sale yourself.

56 – Sew distinctive throw pillows.

You can create unusual throw pillows with distinctive fabric from a fabric store, your home sewing machine, and filler to stuff the pillows with. Sew standard but distinctive pillows for living rooms, pillows with faces on them for kids' rooms, faces with hearts on them for teen girls' rooms, or use your imagination to think of other ways to make your throw pillows distinctive.

57 – Collect for your client and then collect from your client.

Any company that offers its clients credit is a prospect for a collections service. How are you at persuading people to pay their bills…or at least a particular bill? If you can persuade some local businesses that you would be efficient in making collection calls for them, you just might have yourself a gig as a collections solicitor.

Collections agents call both businesses and individuals whose accounts are past due. Keep that in mind when soliciting clients, and don't overlook business-to-business prospects.

58 – Spiders aren't the only ones who design webs.

Website design is a booming business. And you need nothing more in the way of equipment than your home computer and perhaps a software program. Start locally, offering to design a Website (or improve the design of an existing Website) for local businesses. But other than ease of solicitation there's no need to confine your prospects to your local area. You can design a Website just as easily for a client clear across the country.

You need not only a knowledge of HTML *or* a program that does it for you but also a good sense of design and of marketing, since Websites need to do more than just look good. They need to push the client's product or service and make the site easy to navigate.

59 – Offer medical transcription services.

Many doctors today, instead of making notes on each patient's chart, dictate the notes into a pocket tape recorder for a transcription service to type up later. If you're familiar with medical technology you can go into business as a medical transcription service, playing back the tapes and typing up the notes that the doctor dictated.

60 – Not a bookie…a bookkeeper.

One of the most important cogs in the machinery of business is the bookkeeper, but not every business is large enough to need a full-time bookkeeper. Various resolutions to this situation include businesses' hiring a part-time bookkeeper, businesses' hiring one person to do two jobs, one of which is bookkeeping, or even having the boss keep the books after hours.

Another solution is to hire an outside bookkeeping service…and that could be you. Now a small business doesn't need to hire a full-time person for a part-time job, or make this all-important position just one part of the duties of someone who may be better suited to some other position, or pile the work on the boss in the evenings. Now they can just hire your services for a set fee, or by the hour. Your job may include simply data entry of incoming payments and checks written, or it may encompass billing, collection calls, and adjustment of erroneous charges to the firm that hired you.

61 – Be a grants writer.

This is a specialized form of writing and not something you should essay to undertake as a business if you're doing it for the first time. But if you've had previous experience with grants applications, advertise yourself to local nonprofits, educational institutions, and even individuals, and you may be surprised at the quantity of business that turns up.

62 – Audit bills for businesses or individuals.

The two prime areas for your surveillance are phone bills and medical bills. But that's not to preclude your auditing other bills as well.

Both businesses and individuals can benefit from phone bill auditing. The three prime questions for you to ask are: (1) Is your client, whether business or individual, actually receiving every added service that the phone company is billing for? (2) Does your client want, need, and use each of these services? (In some cases, a service such as three-way calling may be available on an as-needed basis for a one-time fee that is lower, if used only a few times a year, than paying for the service monthly.) (3) Is there a combination plan on offer from the phone company that would give your client at a lower package rate all the services now being billed individually? (Sometimes by adding one additional service, even if it's not needed, you can qualify for a package plan that's lower than the current total of individual services.) Additionally, you may want to offer to compare prices of competing phone companies to see if some firm other than the local behemoth can offer a better price.

Medical bills are even more baffling, especially hospital bills, and patients who take the time to peruse them carefully (or have an auditing service do it for them) often discover charges for services not performed.

If you can work your way through the thicket of mysterious charges on medical and/or phone bills, you can offer your clients a real savings and charge them either a flat fee or a percentage of monies saved.

And if you're really good at this financial detective business, you can even consider branching out into auditing other types of bills for businesses.

63 – Mass mailer.

Who sends out mass mailings? Not just "snail spammers" with their "junk mail" that clutters up your mailbox. Homeowner associations, clubs, businesses mailing to clients, churches and synagogues, and other organizations send out large mailings either regularly or irregularly. The envelopes need to be addressed, the contents folded and stuffed in, the postage affixed, the envelopes sealed, and the mailing taken to the Post Office. And *somebody's* got to do all that work.

Why not you?

This is the sort of work that you can involve your whole family in if your kids are eight and ten rather than two and three, and/or that you can hire other SAHMs to help you with.

Some mailings are simply a single letter-sized page; others involve three or five inserts of various sizes. Price your services accordingly. And, yes, you can offer your services to "snail spammers" too. You may hate to be on the receiving end of their mailings, but there's nothing wrong with being on the receiving end of their payments!

64 – Create gift baskets.

Gift baskets are the answer to many an occasion, including: Get Well, Welcome to Your New Home, Congratulations (new baby, first job, major promotion, or other occasions), Good Luck in College, and Bon Voyage. If you can assemble a clever, inventive basket with contents that are particularly suited to the occasion, you can win over new clients and get good word-of-mouth spread about your business.

A basic approach would be to offer just one basket assortment for each of the occasions you wish to handle. Another approach would be to offer two assortments for each occasion, at different prices, which you might call "budget" and "deluxe," or by any other designations you choose. You also might choose to offer two different assortments, one serious and one whimsical. (For example, in a whimsical basket for a first job, you might include an inexpensive clock radio to ensure the recipient getting up in time, and a yo-yo for fighting on-the-job boredom.)

If you have a talent for verse-writing, consider writing a standard poem for each category of basket and including it in each one.

65 – Local merchant representative to new neighbors.

There was a time when anyone who moved into a new residence was visited by a representative of either Welcome Wagon or some similar service. Such in-person visits are rare these days in most parts of the country, though a move may still generate a mailing with coupons from local businesses.

Whether you choose to ring doorbells or simply send out mailings, you can obtain the names of new homeowners or tenants, approach businesses in their area, and either mail or present in person whatever coupons, ads, or other offerings your merchant clients want to put forth.

66 – Be an image consultant.

An image consultant can do her work for an individual or a business and can deal with simply a visual image or with the total image a business puts forth to the public.

Let's start with the smallest scale: the visual image of an individual. After finding out what she wants to say about herself with the way she looks, you can suggest changes in wardrobe, makeup, hairstyle, earrings and other accessories, and eyeglass frames, and can even make suggestions such as your client's using a bronzing gel for a healthier or more outdoorsy look, if you think that will help project the image your client wants.

Now let's look at the other end of the spectrum: corporate image. Here you want to examine a company's name, slogan, logo, stationery, Website, and physical facility. Whether the company is a business located in a traditional office, a retailer in a storefront, an auto dealership, or some other type of entity, if the public visits their facility (as opposed to their doing business entirely by mail order, by phone, or via the Web), what is the first impression potential customers get when they walk in?

Examine, too, the experience of a customer who calls the company: Is he or she greeted by a friendly voice, a harried voice, a recorded voice? Is the "menu" of an automated system customer-friendly and easy to navigate? How long is the average caller kept on hold? Is there music on hold? What type? Does a recording intermittently reassure the caller that he or she hasn't been forgotten? How helpful are the order-takers, customer service reps, or tech reps who will ultimately deal with the customer?

If the company relies heavily on mailings, are they attractive, easy to read, and exciting, and do they put forth the image of the company that the owner wants to promulgate, whether that's friendly and folksy, large and experienced, tech-savvy, budget-minded, luxurious, or otherwise?

In between the visual image of an individual and the total corporate image of a company lies a middle ground as well: the image an individual puts forth of herself or himself not just visually but overall. Do her personality, her voice, her manner of speech and all else about her make her seem intelligent, under-educated, shy, a braggart, competent and in control, uncertain, slovenly, or what? How would she like people to think of her? What changes are within her power to effect in order to better project the image of herself she'd like to put forth?

67 – Medical billing.

Allied to bookkeeping, which we covered earlier, but specialized, medical billing is another field in which there's room for home workers. To do medical billing, in which you bill both individuals and insurance carriers, you need to be conversant with codes for various medical conditions and services.

As a freelance biller, you're not on the doctor's payroll. He or she doesn't need to pay your social security payments, provide space for you in the office, provide a computer for you, or pay your health insurance and other benefits. All these are arguments to persuade doctors' offices to hire your services rather than employ someone in the office to do the job. So when you solicit medical offices for their services, don't overlook soliciting any local doctor's office that's got an ad in the Employment section to hire a biller.

68 – Be a consultant.

What are you knowledgeable about? What career did you have before you became a SAHM? What hobbies are you very well informed about? What did you study in college? What other marketable knowledge do you have?

These are the questions you need to ask yourself before setting yourself up as a consultant. Expand your thinking beyond the narrow scope of your last employed position, to include knowledge you gleaned about the industry you worked in, knowledge you've acquired through volunteer work, and any other subjects you might be particularly well informed about.

Then offer to share that knowledge with others…for a fee.

69 – Be a public speaker.

If you're knowledgeable about a particular subject, are well spoken, and have no fear of standing up in front of groups of people and addressing them, you can share your knowledge with others in groups and derive a fee for doing so. You can speak on a work-related subject that ties in with your former career. You can address parent groups on "Baby-Proofing Your Home" or "Ten Steps You Must Take To Keep Your Child Safe." You can address singles on "How To Meet Your Ideal Mate." You can even speak to other SAHMs on income-earning opportunities for them! What do you know? Share it!

70 – Become a publisher.

If you have a desktop publishing program and know how to use it, you can put out a newsletter or even a newspaper from home. If you've had no previous experience in publishing, better to start small, with a newsletter rather than a newspaper, and with a smaller circulation. Think local rather than national

Be aware that publishers make money in two ways: through sales of copies of the publication and through sales of ads within the publication. The more copies of the newspaper or newsletter you get in the hands of readers, the more you can charge for each ad. You may want to distribute the newsletter for free and make all your money from ad revenue.

Your best bet is to target a specific group, such as parents or senior citizens or college students (if yours is a college town) or pet owners, with news of interest to them. Solicit targeted ads first. For a pet owner's newsletter, for example, you would approach area veterinarians, pet stores, dog groomers, and any services such as dog walkers, pet sitters, people who knit sweaters for dogs, and other related services. Though you can also solicit national brands of dog food and dog toys and other pet-related products (e.g. carrier manufacturers, electronic dog fence manufacturers, pet ID tag manufacturers), you're less likely to be successful in selling to them, though that shouldn't stop you from trying.

And of course there's no reason not to solicit ads from unrelated businesses as well. Dog owners don't spend time 24/7 with their pets. They also go to the movies, rent videos, buy groceries, eat in restaurants, buy clothes...and so any such an establishment could conceivably advertise in your newsletter too. It's just more of a longshot that you'd get them to advertise.

71 – Publish for someone else.

That same desktop publishing software that you'll use for the venture above can come in handy if you put out a newsletter for some other concern. Any local business that has a database of its customers can send out periodic mailings to them, for example. My former veterinarian sent out a newsletter to all her clients semi-regularly, with news and information about pet care, which kept the vet in her clients' minds. Other types of businesses can also send out newsletters to regular or former customers, or to potential customers, whom it can target either by area or by identifying people in a specific group, such as parents of school-age kids, owners of older homes, or people over 62.

Which are you more likely to read: an advertisement from a car dealership, or a newsletter filled with auto care tips, car games you can play with your kids, hints on gas economy, interesting and offbeat automotive-related statistics, info on local road construction…and also information on the latest models available at the dealership?

Then there are employee newsletters, sent not to clients but to workers for a particular concern; organizational newsletters, sent to members; church or synagogue newsletters sent to members, and other similar newsletters. These are not sales tools but are still important means of communication for the business or organization that puts each one out. And *someone* has to write and edit the articles, assemble any ads, and put the whole thing together.

If you offer to write, edit, design, lay out, and possibly also mail these newsletters, you can garner some extra money for yourself. Solicit both those organizations and businesses that already have a newsletter (telling them you can make their newsletter more attractive and do it economically too) and those that don't have one but could profit from one.

72 – Be a broadcaster.

Some radio stations will sell a block of time—a half hour or an hour—to anyone who wants to buy it, produce a show, and sell advertising on it. If you have an interesting concept (perhaps a show aimed at parents?), can create interesting content for it, and are comfortable in front of a microphone, you can line up guests, write interview questions, amass information to share with your listeners, and solicit advertisers by phone and mail, all from the comfort of your home. Only the actual broadcasting and a very few sales calls will require you to be away from home.

73 – Pet sit.

You can make extra money by caring for pets whose owners are going to be away. If you don't want to have to go to the owners' homes twice a day to feed, water, and walk the dog, or change the litter box for the cat or the cage liner for the gerbil, parakeet, or what-have-you, you can take the animal into your home while the owner is gone.

74 – Plant sit.

Just as pets need care while their owners are gone, so do plants. Of course, a plant owner leaving town for just a weekend can usually leave the plants alone. But if she or he is going to be gone for a week or more, those plants are going to need watering.

As with the pets, if you don't want to have to visit the owner's home, you can take them into your own home in the owner's absence, give them sun and water, talk to them, trim off any yellowed leaves, and return them to their owner in good condition when he or she returns.

And get paid for it.

75 – Create your own line of healthy, homemade pet foods.

Most canned dog foods and cat foods have lots of fillers and "by-products" in them. And most of the healthier dog foods and cat foods are of the dry variety, nor are they "natural" or "organic."

For the pet owner who wants his pet to have a healthier diet, particularly if he wants to feed his pet organic and/or "wet" food, the options are limited…and often result in his cooking for the pet himself or settling for something less than optimal.

Familiarize yourself with pet nutritional guidelines and then cook up batches of dog food and cat food, freeze it in single servings, and offer it to local pet owners. Now when the pet owner wants to feed Fido or Fluffy a healthy meal, all she has to do is open a package, nuke the contents, and...voila! Dinner is served.

76 – Knit sweaters for dogs.

Don't overlook Fido (or, rather, his owner) as a customer for your knitting talents. Whether you knit to order or sell pre-knitted sweaters (or do both!), there's money to be made in dog sweaters. You can advertise and sell from home, and/or you can ask local pet shops and even veterinarians if they'd carry your line of pet sweaters on consignment and pay you for each one sold.

77 – Sew or knit dog and cat toys.

From the traditional catnip-filled mouse to more esoteric toys, Rex and Cuddles love to play, and their owners will be happy to pay you for toys for them to play with. Knitting, crocheting, and sewing will all produce suitable toys, although of different sorts. As with the dog sweaters, you can sell these items either from home by way of advertisements or on consignment at local pet stores and veterinarians' offices.

78 – Sew or knit baby toys.

If you can sew or knit pet toys, you can also craft soft, cuddly baby toys. Remember that safety is paramount. Create nothing that might cause a choking hazard or other danger.

You can also crochet stuffed animals for older kids.

79 – Offer in-home dinner service for those who can afford it.

We've already talked about your cooking a week's worth of meals in advance for seniors, the disabled, and the culinary challenged. But this is a little different. This service offers all the advantages of restaurant eating combined with the comforts of home. And it's a one-shot proposition each time.

You either cook the meal at home and then deliver it, hot, to the clients' home, or you cook the meal at the clients' home from scratch. (Which option you choose will depend on such factors as what the meal is, how far you live from the clients, how well equipped their kitchen is, and how long you can manage to be away from your own family.) In either case, the clients do nothing at all toward the dinner prep beyond setting the table. You cook and serve the food—a complete meal. Just how complete it is will depend on the clients' wishes. They may want only a main course, a veggie dish, and a starch. They may want a salad in addition. Or they may request soup and/or an appetizer, and/or dessert.

If you wish, and if you can contrive to be away from home long enough, you can offer to remain there, inconspicuously reading in another room, while they eat, then do the dishes (or at least load the dishwasher) for them when they're finished. Otherwise simply cooking a complete meal is service enough.

80 – Be a wedding consultant.

If you've helped a friend plan a large wedding, planned every detail of your own wedding, or are otherwise knowledgeable about the A to Z of weddings, you can undertake the joyous (if sometimes frustrating) business of being a wedding consultant. Planning not just the reception but the ceremony, the color-coordination of clothes and of decorations…the whole works…you'll be immersed in the happiest of celebrations.

Be warned: It's not all fun. When the bride wants one thing, the bride's mother wants something else, and the bride's future mother-in-law wants a third thing, all of which are contradictory, you'll feel more like a referee or a mediator than a party planner. And when the bride is insistent on what adds up to fully twice the budget she's prepared to spend, be ready for tears. (I meant the bride's…but yours may follow.)

Still, overall it's a happy job—and one that pays. And it's one that can be largely undertaken from home via phone calls.

81 – Be a makeup artist.

Makeup artists basically do two different things: They revamp a woman's look by changing the way she uses makeup, and they make women up for special occasions such as weddings, fancy parties, and even job interviews, and for TV appearances (most local shows don't have staff makeup artists) or photo sessions. (Whether you're posing for glamour shots, professional pictures, or family portraits, you want to look your best.)

As a makeup artist, you'll need to know about the different kinds of makeup, contouring and highlights, complementary shades, and more. You'll need an arsenal of makeup and a makeup table with good light.

To advise a client about how to use makeup in general, you'll need to know something about her: How does she see herself, personality-wise, and how does she want the rest of the world to view her? How does she usually dress? What is her job? What is her lifestyle—active and smudge-prone, often out in the rain or sun, or relatively protected? How willing is she to take the time and trouble to put on an extensive amount of makeup for everyday use? Are special occasions frequent or rare in her life?

To make up a client for a special occasion, of course you'll need to know if you're putting on makeup to be seen by the eye of a camera (heavier makeup) or in person (a more natural look). You will need to know, too, if she will be seen primarily in daylight, in fluorescent light, or in incandescent light. And of course the client should be wearing the clothes (and any wig, or hat) that she will be dressed in, so you can choose colors that will work best with her clothing color, hair color, and hat color.

82 – Start a small PR agency.

Public relations is not the same as advertising, of course. You'll primarily be writing and sending out press releases, though there's a lot more to PR than just that. Depending on who your clients are and how large their budgets are, you may be trying to book them on local radio and TV shows, trying to book them into local live events (e.g. trying to secure a spot for a doctor in a health fair that's being held for the public, or trying to involve the director of a daycare center in a Family Fun Fest at the local mall), trying to get them interviewed by local columnists or reporters, or even trying to get them national exposure. You may even be asked to put together an event yourself, if your clients include a hospital or a shopping center, to cite just two examples.

83 – Be a résumé writer.

There's more to writing a résumé than just listing your past jobs. What sort of résumé a job prospect offers may make the difference between her getting a second interview or not…or her getting the job or not. If you can craft a good résumé, you can charge for your services.

Hint: If you happen to live in an area where there's an active theatrical industry (live theatre, movies, or TV), remember that actors and actresses need résumés too.

84 – Offer secretarial support.

Nowadays, with so much correspondence accomplished by Email, the days of "Miss Jones, take a letter" are fading fast. Fewer letters are sent by "snail-mail," more big bosses do their own typing than previously, and fewer secretaries are out there than before.

Often, if someone does type a letter for a higher-up, her or his title isn't "secretary" but perhaps "administrative assistant" or "assistant to the manager" or some such.

In some offices, there isn't anyone to do the work of typing a letter for the higher-ups, and if they have to do it themselves, the letter may be typo-laden.

You can hire out your secretarial services under any of a number of arrangements. Your client can dictate a letter to you by phone. Your client can tell you the circumstances and leave it to you to compose the letter. Or your client can provide you with certain form letters that you store on your computer and print out, personalized, on request.

Your client may provide you with company letterhead to print out on, or you might have the company's letterhead design stored on your computer, "pasting" it at the top of the document before you type. You might even key in the letter on your home computer, then upload it as an Email attachment to your client for him or her to print it out in his office. (That way he can sign it himself instead of your signing for him.)

85 – Be a business broker.

A business broker puts together people who want to sell businesses and those who want to buy them. And she collects a percentage of the eventual selling price as her fee. You'll need to meet with each client at least once, but the bulk of your business can be done by phone. You'll need to advertise aggressively, but that will constitute your only major outlay of money.

If you don't mind having your clients meet with you in a home office, and you have someplace more businesslike than the dining room table for them to sit, they can meet with you in your house, though in the case of the sellers, you'll want to see the actual place of business once.

86 – Decorate wall mirrors for that unusual yet attractive touch.

With plain mirrors, either bought new or bought at secondhand furniture stores, and a bit of decoration, you can turn out creations that both adults and teen girls will want for their rooms. If the mirror is from a secondhand furniture store, it probably has a wooden frame. You can glue the decoration onto the frame. If the mirror is a new, inexpensive mirror, it probably has only a thin, functional (non-decorative) metal frame, and you'll glue the decoration around the edge of the mirror.

Depending on your choice of decoration, you can make the mirror suitable for a bedroom or for a living room, dining room, or hallway. Some decorating possibilities include seashells, small artificial flowers, gilt paint, sequins, and small squares of colored mosaic-type tile.

87 – Party house.

There's a party on Saturday…and it's at your house. It isn't anyone's actual birthday, but there'll be ice cream and cake, games, goodie bags, and general merriment for a couple of hours. Instead of every attendee bringing a present for the honoree, though, they'll bring an admission fee for the hostess. That's you, of course.

Depending on how large the kid population is in your area, you can hostess a party every weekend, once a month, or at some other interval.

You can also host parties for the actual birthday of any child whose mom would rather pay you to buy the cake, supervise the guests, clean up afterward, and organize the games and other events. Your price list can start with just a basic party as I've described above and, for an extra fee, include a clown, or a magician, or a rented bounce house, or a rented cotton candy machine, or whatever else you wish to make an option.

88 – Babysitter training.

Offer an intensive three-hour course for babysitters, complete with a certificate awarded to those who take and complete the course. The course should teach rules of safety, rules of babysitter etiquette, CPR, the Heimlich maneuver, and basic first aid, suitable games the sitters can play with their charges, and a list of questions a sitter should always ask the parents (such as whom to call in an emergency, what the kids are allergic to and what health situations they may have, what their bedtime is, what house rules the sitter should know about concerning the TV and anything else the kids may be restricted regarding, where the parents can be reached, and what time they're expected home).

Depending on the number of teenage girls (and boys who want to be sitters) in your area, you can offer the course weekly or monthly.

89 – Be a Senior Sunshine caller.

In every community—yours, mine, all of them—there are senior citizens who get out of the house very little, who live alone, and who may not have many friends left to talk to, or any relatives living nearby. They need a friendly word. And they need to be checked on to make sure they're okay. That famous commercial showing a woman calling, "Help. I've fallen. And I can't get up" makes a good case not only for the product it advertises but for checking on seniors in general. What if an elder woman has fallen and isn't wearing one of those things? What if an elder man has fallen because he passed out, and being unconscious, he can't activate the device? What if he's conscious but has had a stroke and can't move or speak?

Or what if he or she is still fine…so far…but is lonely and just needs an uplifting Hello?

For a nominal monthly fee (paid either by the senior citizen or by his or her family), you call him or her daily, make sure he's all right, call back later if there's no answer. (He might just have a doctor's appointment or be in his backyard.) And call a relative or a neighbor with a key if there's any question. Assuming you do reach the senior and talk to him or her by phone, talk for a few minutes. Cheer him up. Keep him company. Your voice may be the only one he hears today that doesn't emanate mechanically from a TV, radio, or stereo. Even if all he talks about is how his arthritis is kicking up, and even though these aren't the cheeriest of phone calls for you to make, you'll know you've made a real difference in someone's life. And that should make you feel good.

90 – Offer budget and/or credit counselling.

Many people just don't know how to budget their money. Others haven't got a good grasp of how to manage their credit.

They'll pay down a low-interest loan before a high-interest credit card, or fail to realize that a low-interest home equity loan could pay off a high-interest card, or simply think that, because they've not yet maxed out their cards, they're okay, heedless of how much they're paying monthly in interest.

Do you have a good grasp of numbers, a good sense of how to budget, some knowledge of credit options, and perhaps the ability to bargain with a creditor to effect a settlement in which a partial payment is accepted as payment in full? Then you can offer budget counselling and/or credit counselling. You'll truly help someone who needs help…and you can feel justified in charging them for that help. You're saving them way more than you're costing them.

91 – Provide tape duplication service.

Most people can dupe audio tapes or at least have a friend who has a dual-deck stereo, but videotapes are trickier. Not that many people by comparison have two VCRs. There are plenty of non-copyrighted tapes that people want duplicated: wedding videos, pictures of the kids, which the grandparents on both sides of the family are clamoring for, footage of your client's appearance on TV, and more. Without breaking any copyright laws you can still duplicate tapes for a fee.

92 – Create one-of-a-kind designer perfumes.

If you have a good nose and a collection of essential oils (the basis of perfumes), you can create a distinctive designer fragrance for each of your clients, a scent that's hers alone. (Be sure to keep track of the formula, so you can duplicate it when the customer needs more!)

93 – Be a dispute mediator.

Not every dispute winds up in court…and not every dispute winds up being settled amicably, either. In between those two extremes lie disputes of all kinds—between neighbors, between friends and relatives, even business disputes too trivial to sue over and yet disturbing nonetheless. Often the disputants would be willing to listen to the decision of an uninvolved third party if they could find one they both believed fair-minded.

Might that be you?

You can listen to both sides of the story, render a decision…and charge (before handing down your decision!) for your service.

94 – Be a practical life advisor.

Sometimes people need more advice than their friends can give them. Or they don't want their friends to know their troubles. Or their friends are wonderful people but not the most level-headed.

These are the times that people write to newspaper advice columnists. But not every columnist answers every question she or he gets. And when they do answer, it often takes weeks. Sometimes people in a jam need help sooner than that.

There are certain areas you shouldn't offer paid advice in. If a person has a legal problem, you can't practice law without a license and advise them. If a person is seriously emotionally disturbed, or seems suicidal, they certainly need help from a professional in the field of mental health. There are other areas, too, in which it's best you don't tread. But that still leaves an awful lot of ground for you to cover.

You can feel good about knowing you're making money by genuinely helping someone.

95 – Be a modern-day bard.

Selling poetry to magazines, or collections of poetry to book publishers, is not the way to wealth. And writing greeting card verse for card companies is a tough sell too. But you can sell on a one-to-one basis…and while you won't get rich this way either, you'll probably sell more of your poetry.

Who can you sell it to? Mostly to lovers—courting or married. But verses for kids with their own names worked into the poems are a good birthday bet. And graduations, adult birthdays, retirement, or most any other occasion can bring their share of orders too.

You can write poems without greeting cards being involved—just poems hand-written on paper, or typed on computer (perhaps in a script font), or delivered to the customer to be recopied in his or her own handwriting. (Yes, some of your customers are going to take credit for your creations. Live with it.

You've got the cash.) You can also sell poems hand-written into blank greeting cards.

As well as poems, you can write non-poetic greeting card sentiments (still called "verse" in the trade, but they're not actually poems), or letters expressing a lover's true feelings, or a mother's pride, or a daughter's appreciation, or the feelings of anyone else who isn't wonderful at putting into words the sentiment he or she wants to express.

Valentine's Day is likely to be your busiest time, but business will trickle in at other times too.

96 – "Dyeing" to make some money? Decorate T-shirts that fit to a T!

If you have a flair for design and can decorate T-shirts, buy some plain, unadorned T-shirts (white or colored) in popular sizes (hint: men's Xtra-Large shirts also double as women's nightshirts), and spiff them up with fabric paints, or tie-dyeing, or even with sequins or appliques or small beads, and sell your wearable art at a profit. Buy in bulk (for bulk discount) to effect greater savings…and greater profits.

97 – Sell your old clothes.

Instead of giving away your children's good-condition outgrown clothes to friends as hand-me-downs, offer them for sale. A local consignment shop that specializes in children's things (or in clothes for all the family) is your best bet, though a yard sale will do if there's no such consignment shop in your area, or if the clothes you're offering are in less-than-wonderful condition.

You can also collect clothes from your friends and sell them too. Offer a share of the profits. (Ultimately this could lead to your opening a consignment shop yourself.)

98 – Instead of donating your no-longer-wanted books and other items, resell them.

You can also offer to resell your friends' items and share the profits with them. This can be something as small as a book, as large as a big piece of furniture.

99 – Create spice blends, barbeque sauces, and marinades.

There's an ever-growing market for barbeque sauces and marinades, and spice blends get some attention too. You can create your own gastronomic flavor-enhancers and market them, advertising locally or on the Web, or selling by mail, or selling to local stores.

100 – Create and sell decorative candles.

These may be traditional candles in a marbled wax pattern, or in unusual colors, or they may be candles in bowls or in other presentation rather than traditional candlesticks. One local artisan in my area crafts candles in irregular sort-of-round shapes with sand and seashells glued to the outside. Candles are for more than just romantic candlelit dinners (or emergency use during power outages). A candle lit on a coffee table (with the ambient lighting on low) really graces a home.

If your kids are little, you may not think in terms of candles because of the risk involved, but plenty of people who don't have little kids would love to have and use decorative candles.

101 – Write a book.

If you have knowledge on a subject to share with others, consider turning it into a book. Writing the book is easier than selling it to a publisher. Trust me, it isn't that easy to get a book published. But thousands of books are published every year, and yours could well be one of them. (Or you could self-publish, provided you have a viable means of distribution and sales.)

Whether your book is of interest to weekend gardeners, parents, home cooks, pet lovers, kids, vegetarians, astrology buffs, or celebrity-watchers, if you have knowledge that will be of interest to a particular group of people, share it. If you can write well and present useful and/or interesting information, there may be a market for your book.

Like this one.

Before You Get Started

By now, hopefully you've picked one (or more!) ideas that appeal to you as a means of making money. But before you rush headlong into your venture, there are a few things you need to do first:

1 – Are you going to be getting phone calls from prospective clients? I hope your three-year-old doesn't answer your phone! And if your ten-year-old does, make sure he understands that Mom is going to be getting business calls, and he needs to answer the phone appropriately and, if you're not available, to take messages faithfully and accurately…and to always put the messages in a designated spot.

That spot might be a corkboard complete with pushpins, a file tray such as you can buy at an office supply store, or whatever works best for you. But pick a place for your messages and instruct *any* family member who might take a message for you (this includes your husband!) as to where to put all messages.

2 – In most cases you also need a designated work space or file space. If you've chosen to be a clown entertainer for children's parties, you may not think this calls for any kind of work space at home, but it does. You need somewhere to store bills for makeup and other business expenses, somewhere (probably on the computer) to store information on parties you've worked at and leads for potential future customers, somewhere to store the business cards you'll hand out to the parents of kids who are guests at the parties you entertain at, leave on counters in local stores, and just hand out in general, and somewhere to store your clown outfits and makeup.

3 – Depending on the nature of your venture, you may want a business name. If you're baking cakes and other edibles, you may just want to use your own name—let's say it's Gwen Jones. But you may want something more professional sounding, like Goodies by Gwen, or Cake Heaven, or Simply Yummy.

4 – Depending on the venture you've settled on and depending on your local laws and regulations, you might need a business license. Chances are you don't, but some localities require professional licensing for such occupations as tutoring or tailoring.

5 – For many ventures, you need to advertise in some way—even if it's just word of mouth. If you're recycling clothes to

a consignment shop, of course you don't need to advertise. But if you're planning birthday parties, baking, or organizing people's closets or offices, for example, you need to let potential customers know that you're available. You can spread the word various ways that are reasonably affordable:

- Put up flyers on bulletin boards in local stores
- Pass out flyers by hand or leave them in people's doors. (Leaving them in mailboxes is not legal.)
- Take an ad in the local paper, the local Pennysaver, the newsletter of any suitable local organization, the newsletter of any suitable local homeowners' association, or whatever other opportunities your area offers.
- Have business cards printed to hand out to anyone you meet, to all potential clients, and to anyone else who might help. Give several to your existing clients so they can give them to friends. Leave some at local stores and other businesses that are willing to let you display them. Post them on community bulletin boards. Trade a bunch of cards with someone who is in a related field. (For example, if you're creating artificial flower arrangements for offices, trade cards with someone who sets up or services office aquariums or waters plants in commercial venues.)

6 – You may want to work out a babysitting trade arrangement with another SAHM, whether or not she's got a money-making venture going. You can watch her kids three hours every Friday, one hour every morning, or on an as-needed basis in return for similar coverage of your kids from her. This will give you time to engage in work pursuits without having to keep one ear out for your two-year-old, or go out on business calls without your infant strapped to your chest.